London Borough of Tower Hamlets

91000008122684

D1759886

THE LAST YEARS OF LONDON'S RFS AND RTs: NORTH OF THE THAMES

MIKE RHODES

AMBERLEY

Bibliography

Blacker, Ken, *RT The Story of a London Bus* (London: Capital Transport Publishing, 1979)
Joyce, J., *London Transport Bus Garages since 1948* (London: Ian Alan Ltd, 1988)

First published 2021

Amberley Publishing
The Hill, Stroud
Gloucestershire, GL5 4EP

www.amberley-books.com

Copyright © Mike Rhodes, 2021

The right of Mike Rhodes to be identified as
the Author of this work has been asserted in
accordance with the Copyrights, Designs and
Patents Act 1988.

ISBN 978 1 3981 0350 4 (print)
ISBN 978 1 3981 0351 1 (ebook)

All rights reserved. No part of this book may be
reprinted or reproduced or utilised in any form
or by any electronic, mechanical or other means,
now known or hereafter invented, including
photocopying and recording, or in any information
storage or retrieval system, without the permission
in writing from the Publishers.

British Library Cataloguing in Publication Data.
A catalogue record for this book is available from
the British Library.

Origination by Amberley Publishing.
Printed in the UK.

Introduction

Many books have been written about these two iconic stalwarts of London Transport's history – and quite rightly so. The single-deck AEC Regal IV (RF) and the double-deck AEC Regent III (RT) played a principal part in the workings of London's route network for close on three decades, from the late 1940s through to the mid-1970s. This account concentrates on their final years and the routes they operated to the north of the River Thames. The period covered is from around the beginning of 1976 through to the final demise of the RTs at the beginning of April 1979. By this time the RT had all but been eliminated from central London, with only routes 109, 155 and 176/176^A still scheduled to be regularly operated by the type, with the last of these succumbing in October of that year. However, Barking still turned out a handful of RTs for two nocturnal N-prefixed routes until mid-1978.

This is a personal account put together from the author's own collection of photographs taken over this period and supplemented by pictures taken by his associate of many years Dr Ian Derrick, who accompanied him on a number of his trips to the metropolis.

The RT story began way back in 1938 when the Chiswick think tank was charged with designing a new 'standard' London bus. RT1 was the result, which comprised an AEC-designed chassis powered by a 9.6-litre diesel engine and fitted with an in-house built fifty-five-seat double-deck body. One of the innovative features of this bus was the sliding cab door, which would remain a feature of London Transport's double-deck buses for the next thirty years. RT1 entered service from Putney's Chelverton Road garage on 17 June 1939. After initial testing and some modifications authorisation was given to build a further 150 of the type, which became Nos RT2–151. Mechanically, these were similar to RT1 but the body, again built in-house, was of an integral construction. Whereas RT1 had received an all-metal body, the first production batch had bodies that incorporated wood-metal frames. They were 26 ft long x 14 ft 3½ ins high and were fitted with fifty-six seats (with one additional seat having been fitted on the upper deck). The majority of the batch had been placed in service by June 1940, but with the onslaught of the Second World War the last five trickled into service between March 1941 and February 1942.

Following the cessation of hostilities, it was decided that with a few refinements the RT class should be built in large numbers. The major change in design was the reversion to an all-metal frame. While the chassis were again built by AEC the bodies were constructed by four separate bodybuilders – namely Park Royal, Weymann, Cravens and Saunders-Roe. One prominent feature of the early deliveries was the provision of a roof-mounted route number box, which was later discontinued. History also deemed that the Weymann and Park Royal-constructed bodies were far superior to the other two, as these were eliminated from the fleet by as early as October 1957 (Cravens) and March 1971 (Saunders-Roe). As with the RT's successor, the Routemaster, a degree of swapping of body types took place when the buses passed through Aldenham Works for overhaul. The last major overhauls of the type were undertaken in 1970.

Construction of the RT bus eventually resumed in 1947 and continued without a break until 1954 when production finally came to an end. By then there was actually a surplus of buses and a number of the last batch of Weymann-bodied vehicles were initially put into store before being placed into service in the country area between 1955 and 1958. In all, 4,674 post-war Regents were built over an eight-year period, with around 870 initially joining the green-painted country fleet. Over the following years some buses were swapped between the country and central areas and vice versa. At the same time buses of a similar design but mounted on Leyland chassis, designated as the RTL and RTW, were also being constructed, but the last of these were withdrawn by the end of 1970 and are not part of this story.

At the beginning of the 1970s there was still in excess of 3,300 RTs in service, and together with the RMs they dominated the central area routes but, with the implementation of 'OPO' and the introduction of Daimler Fleetlines and AEC Merlins and Swifts in some numbers, under the LT Reshaping Plan this figure had dropped dramatically by January 1976. The remaining routes throughout the network scheduled for RT operation on Mondays to Fridays required 640 buses, with 275 of these being allocated to ten garages in the north to work twenty-three different routes (the 175 and 217^B were later added to these, with buses also being provided for two additional routes on Sunday only). These were distributed as follows (conversion dates in parenthesis):

AC	Willesden	9	176 (11/3/76)
AD	Palmers Green	32	34 (10/9/77), 102 (1/2/78), 261 (4/3/78)
AP	Seven Kings	56	86 (28/2/76), 129 (9/10/76), 139 (23/7/77), 148 (23/7/77), 150 (15/10/77), 193 (19/3/77)
BK	Barking	52	62 (7/4/79), 87 (28/10/78), 148 (23/7/77), N95 (26/5/78), N98 (26/5/78)
BN*	Brixton		109 (23/5/76)
E	Enfield	21	135 (16/1/78), 135^A (20/8/77), 205 (SuO) (10/4/76), 217 (20/8/77), 217^B (20/8/77)
HD	Harrow Weald	28	140 (15/7/78)
HW	Southall	34	105 (30/4/78), 120 (28/1/78), 274 (1/10/77)
L	Loughton	18	20A (9/10/76), 167^A (10/4/76), 205^A (SuO) (10/4/76), 217^A (20/8/77)
NS	Romford	11	139 (23/7/77), 175 (19/3/77), 247 (24/4/76)
S	Shepherds Bush	7	105 (30/4/78)
TH*	Thornton Heath		109 (3/10/76)
WL*	Walworth		176 (21/3/76), 176^A (21/3/76)
WW	Walthamstow	11	34 (10/9/77)

* Southern Area Garages

The highest concentrations of the type could therefore be seen in Barnet and Enfield in the north; Barking, Dagenham, Goodmayes, Ilford and Romford in the east; and Harrow, Hounslow and Southall in the west. Seven Kings still had a 100 per cent allocation of Regents brought about by the somewhat restricted nature of the confines of the garage. Following a protracted rebuilding programme, the RTs were replaced with other types between February 1976 and October 1977. It is well documented that Barking garage was the last to operate the type and extensive coverage is given to the last two routes, culminating with the activities that were played out on the final day.

Records show that there were just forty-four green examples still licensed for service at the start of the period under review, of which only sixteen were based in the north; of these, six were allocated to Garston and four to Windsor. By the following year these had been reduced to nine, with the last two operational RTs, Nos 3636 and 3752, being withdrawn from Garston garage the following

April. The southern area fared a little better, with Chelsham retaining seventeen and Leatherhead seven; these could principally be found working on routes 403 and 406 at Croydon and Kingston respectively. Two of these made it into 1978, with RT1018 lasting until May and, last of all, RT604 continuing until September. Both of these Regents had received NBC leaf-green livery.

As the 1950s took hold and the new family of RTs began to settle down on the central area routes, the design team turned their attention to producing a standard single-deck type that could be used on some of the outlying central area routes, but more particularly in the country area and on the expanding Green Line network of cross-city routes. With the chassis again built by AEC and based on the Regal IV marque, the initial twenty-five buses (RF1–25) were fitted with thirty-five-seat, Metro-Cammell-built bodies and designated as 'private hire' buses. They were first allocated to seven central area garages between April and June 1951. The whole batch was later refurbished for use on Green Line services. The next 263 buses (RF26–288), which were fitted with thirty-nine-seat bodies (with the length having been extended from 27½ to 30 ft), were allocated from new to the Green Line services over a twelve-month period from October 1951. Next to benefit were some of the central area routes, with the introduction of a further 225 vehicles (RF289–513) painted in central area red. These were fitted out with forty-one seats, but did not have doors – at the insistence of the Metropolitan Police. The final 187 machines (RF514–700) of this 700-strong class were allocated to country area garages, with the last entering service in December 1953. Over the ensuing years a certain amount of renumbering and transfer of buses between divisions took place. Additionally, the central area buses were later fitted with doors and equipped for 'OPO'. Of the 137 red RFs scheduled for service on Monday to Friday, at the start of 1976 only fifty-two were required in the north. These were distributed as follows (conversion dates in parenthesis):

AD	Palmers Green	5	212 (21/3/76)
E	Enfield	4	121 (24/10/76)
EW	Edgware	12	251 (30/1/77)
L	Loughton	7	254 10/4/76)
NS	Romford	4	250 (24/4/76)
R	Riverside	4	290 (9/5/76)
UX	Uxbridge	16	223 (12/12/76), 224 (12/12/76), 224[B] (12/12/76)

As can be seen from the above list, the red RF had been eliminated north of the river by the end of January 1977. Indeed, by the end of that April only the 218 and 219 at Kingston in the south continued to be operated by RFs. This situation was destined to continue for almost a further two years as no suitable bus was available to replace the remaining examples, due mainly to the constraints of Kingston bus garage. In order to cope with the situation London Transport took the somewhat unusual step of recertifying twenty-five Regals in 1977/8, with the work being undertaken at Stonebridge Park and Hanwell garages.

Meanwhile, of the combined Green Line and country area buses only around seventy survived in service until 1976. These were used on a variety of routes from a number of garages throughout the London Country operating area, usually deputising for more modern types. The last original country RF to be withdrawn was RF684 at Chelsham in May 1978, the only one of the type to remain in use after September 1977, while the last two former Green Line examples were RF221 at Chelsham and RF202 at Northfleet, which were withdrawn in March and July 1979 respectively.

The pictures featured in this account were largely taken using a Kodak Pocket Instamatic 60 camera, which was fitted with a F2.7 26-mm Ektar lens. Shutter speed varied from 10 seconds to 1/250th of a second, with a focal range of 3 ft to Infinity. The camera was designed for use with Kodakcolor or Kodachrome 110 cartridge film, which produced 16-mm negatives or transparencies. The actual camera used is illustrated here.

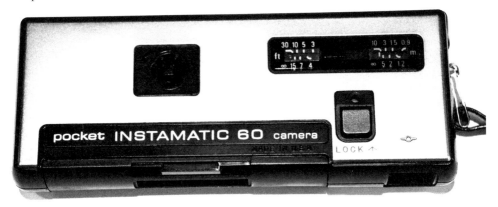

With the advance of scanners it has been possible to scan the original negatives and transparencies using an Epson Perfection V700 scanner. The scans of these forty-year-old originals were cleaned up and the colours restored using the Photoshop Element 9 programme. It must be appreciated that, with the small size of the original negatives, some of the pictures may have lost a little clarity when enlarged, although the lens fitted to the camera was deemed to be of excellent quality for the type of camera when it was first introduced in 1972. Photographs provided by Dr Derrick were taken using an Olympus Trip camera, which was fitted with a 40-mm F2 lens with a maximum shutter speed of 1/200th of a second, using 35-mm Kodachrome transparency film and are denoted as thus: (ID).

The author would like to acknowledge reference to the websites maintained by Ian Armstrong and Ian Smith with regards to the vehicle requirements for London bus routes and information relating to London Transport buses and to the RED-RF website maintained by Peter Osborn.

The following abbreviations have been used a number of times throughout the book: AEC – Associated Equipment Company, LGOC – London General Omnibus Company, LCBS – London Country Bus Services, LT – London Transport, NBC – National Bus Company, 'OPO' – One Person Operated, PH – Public House, PSV – Passenger Service Vehicle.

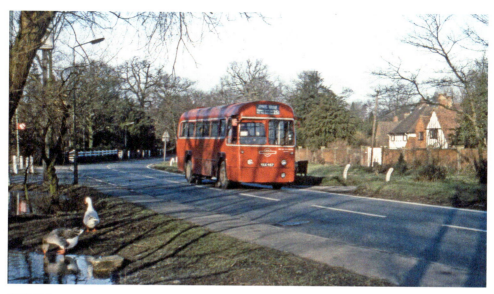

EW Edgware

Route 251 first gained an RF allocation on 6 May 1953, on Saturdays only. Gradually the type replaced the Leyland Tiger PS1 TDs, with full conversion being completed in May 1957. The route was converted to 'OPO' from 27 January 1965. Muswell Hill garage had provided the buses until February 1963 when operation was transferred to Edgware. Latterly fourteen buses were scheduled on Mon–Fri, with seven on Saturday and four on Sundays. These two views date from Saturday 29 January 1977 and depict RF510 (above) and RF518 (below) passing Totteridge Village Green. New Bristol LH Types (BL) took over operation of the route from the following day. Both of these RFs saw further service at Kingston before bowing out. The route was still operated in 2021 by London Sovereign using Alexander Dennis Enviros.

The 251 essentially ran from Stanmore station to Arnos Grove station via Mill Hill and Totteridge & Whetstone. RF503 is seen at Arnos Grove on 8 October 1976. The station frontage is a Grade II listed building and was originally a terminus of the Piccadilly Line, which was opened on 19 September 1932. The line was extended to Oakwood six months later before reaching Cockfosters in July 1933.

E Enfield

Enfield garage, also known as Ponders End, was opened by the LGOC in 1927. By 1976 the allocation of buses largely consisted of Daimler Fleetlines (DMS) and Regent RTs. The latter were still employed on local services 135, 135[A] and 217[B], and the 217, which took them a little further afield. Additionally, the 205 required three buses on a Sunday until the route was withdrawn in April 1976. Enfield also had a small allocation of RMs for the 279 and Ford Transit FSs for the W9. Reposing on the garage forecourt on 29 January 1977 were RT Nos 3814, 4627 and 3101. The layout was much the same in 2021 but fenced off.

On 4 June 1977, RT2173 is pursued by London Country Atlantean AN97 along The Town (Church Street) in the centre of Enfield. Services 135 and 135^A were local to the area and basically followed the same route between Carterhatch and Brimsdown station. Two months later RT2173 was transferred to Seven Kings. The Bakers Oven later became a Rymans store.

RT3101 is seen on the same day pulling away from the Glyn Road bus stop, which was opposite the garage in Southbury Road. The combined service required ten buses on Mon–Fri. The two services were integrated on 20 August 1977 and the resultant 135 was converted to Routemaster operation on 16 January 1978 ('OPO' with DMSs had been introduced on Sundays from April 1974).

RT1551 is displaying the 135 service number as it pauses in Brimsdown Avenue, alongside Brimsdown station, before setting off back to Carterhatch. It was captured on 8 October 1976, only three months before it was withdrawn and sold to E. H. Brakell of Cheam. The route had originally been introduced in February 1942 and had achieved nearly forty years of operation when it was withdrawn in December 1981.

Route 217^B only came into being on 10 April 1976 and may well have been the last new central area route to receive the RT type. RT4627 is seen at Ninefields North on 8 October 1976 where the houses were still being built. Only four buses were required on Mon–Fri, although the Sunday timetable was also crew-operated. DMS Fleetlines took over on 20 August 1977, with the route largely being absorbed by the new 317 in 1987.

Enfield garage was also responsible for providing buses for the lengthy 217 service, which ran from Waltham Cross to Turnpike Lane station. RT4316, seen passing the Queens Head PH in Paternoster Hill at Upshire on Friday 8 October 1976, was one of nine RTs employed on the route on that day of the week.

On a Saturday only six buses were required for the 217. RT Nos 1876, 1989 and 1572 are seen parked in Hartsway, alongside the garage building, on 4 June 1977. By 2021 this thoroughfare had been absorbed into the garage complex. With the conversion of the 217/217^B services to 'OPO' two months later, all three buses were moved on to Plumstead garage, with just the 135 allocation remaining until January 1978.

Little and large: Sixteen-seat Ford Transit FS9 was one of four of the type allocated to Enfield to work the W9 service. When seen on 4 June 1977 this bus had already done the rounds, having been successively allocated to Bromley (B1 service), Enfield (W9), Stockwell (P4) and Potters Bar (PB1). It was sold to Ensignbus in January 1980. Alongside is RT953, which moved to Poplar and then Southall two months later.

RF531 is seen in Southall Road in Enfield approaching journey's end on 8 October 1976. The 121 was somewhat unusual in having a sub-200 route number and being operated by the Regal IVs, presumably because it had been double-deck worked until 1966. Just four buses were required to operate this east–west service on Mon–Fri, which reverted to double-deck operation with DMS Fleetlines two weeks after this picture was taken.

RF526 is also seen in Enfield on 8 October 1976. The location is Cecil Road, an area of the town that has since changed dramatically following the construction of the Palace Exchange Shopping Centre. This Regal saw further service at Edgware and finally Kingston before being sold to C. F. Booth at Rotherham for scrap in November 1978.

HD Harrow Weald

Harrow Weald garage had been solely responsible for the Mon–Sat allocation of buses on route 140 since October 1962. Running from Mill Hill Broadway to London Airport (Heathrow) it still required a weekday allocation of twenty-eight RTs at the beginning of 1978. RT3220, which would later see out its days at Bromley, is seen at the airport on Sunday 23 April 1978 in the company of RT4721 from Southall garage on the 105 (ID).

RT2143 is seen departing the airport bus station on the same day on its long journey to Mill Hill. On a Sunday the allocation was for nine RTs from Harrow Weald and three RMLs from Hendon. RT2143 also eked out its last service days at Bromley before acting as a skid bus at Chiswick and lastly being reported as exported to Kobe in Japan in May 1988 (ID).

The 140 passed through a number of high-density local shopping areas on its journey to and from Mill Hill. Passengers clamour to board RT1063 in Watling Avenue at Burnt Oak on 11 March 1978. Largely unchanged in 2021, this section of the route was no longer served from April 1983 when the northern terminus was cut back to Harrow Weald.

The various highway authorities throughout the country always erred on the side of caution when displaying headroom signs on bridges. RT651 would now have 3 inches less clearance (although it is unlikely that the road surface level has been altered) if it was still employed on the 140 in 2021. It is seen passing under the Piccadilly Line in Northolt Road at South Harrow on 27 May 1978.

Also seen at South Harrow, but travelling in the opposite direction on the same day, is RT744. This Regent moved to Bexleyheath for a few more months of service until the end of the year. Forty years later and the electrical appliance shop had become Colorama Imaging Specialists.

RT1303 is seen waiting time in Station Road at Harrow-on-the-Hill on 2 June 1977 before starting out on its journey to the airport. Later fitted with a Weymann body, RT1303 was new in January 1950 with a Saunders roofbox body. Its time at HD was somewhat short as it was sold to Wombwell Diesels for scrap five months later. Leigh Fabrics later became a Thompson Travel shop before that company went into administration in 2019.

RT4313 is seen on the airport stand on 9 October 1976 before the bus station was remodelled. It also went for scrap around the same time as RT1303. The 140 was somewhat hastily converted to Routemaster operation on 15 July 1978. After over sixty years of carrying passengers to the airport the route was cut back to Hayes & Harlington station in December 2019.

Another of Harrow Weald's Regent workhorses, RT848, is seen in the urban setting of Watling Avenue at Burnt Oak on 11 March 1978. This southbound journey is only going as far as Harrow. The route was altered to start at Harrow in April 1983. Note the K6-style red telephone kiosk on the extreme right, which has since been replaced with a more modern KX version.

FW Fulwell

Between 1962 (206)/1966 (264) and 1976 Fulwell garage provided RFs for these two routes, both of which were converted to Bristol LH operation in the summer of their final year. There was also an association with route 201 on Sat/Sun from May 1973. On a Sunday in August 1974 most of the allocation was parked up, including RF Nos 517 (ex-298), 490, 537 and 535 (ID).

AV Hounslow

Hounslow garage was still working the 202 and 237 services with RFs in 1976. The 237 ran from Hounslow bus station to Chertsey station, which took it just south of the Thames. RF385 has a small queue waiting to board for the run down to Chertsey on 9 October 1976. It would not make many more trips as the bus was withdrawn the following month. The bus station no longer has a roof.

RF428 waits in Chertsey station yard for its return departure time to Hounslow, a journey that was scheduled to take around fifty minutes, on 4 December 1976. The twenty-four-year reign of the type on this route came to an end on 17 April 1977 when Bristol LHs took over. The building behind the bus was occupied by OnTheMove Software in 2019 while the bus stand then hosted a manual car wash business.

Another view taken on 9 October 1976 sees RF511 at the Islay Gardens bus stop in Staines Road at Hounslow Heath with a short working to Sunbury village. The Saturday allocation was for nine buses, only one fewer than on Mon–Fri. From 28 January 1978 the route was recast to run from Shepherd's Bush to Sunbury village using RMs.

Earlier in the day RF509 was captured at the Richmond Dee Road terminus of route 202. RFs had only been introduced to the route in September 1971, taking over from RTs, with just four buses required on a Saturday. The 202 also succumbed to new Bristol LHs in April 1977 when Hounslow lost its RF allocation.

RF603 is seen crossing Richmond Bridge on its return trip to Hounslow on 26 March 1977. The bridge originally dates from 1777 and is a Grade I listed structure. It was widened on the upstream side over the period 1937–40 when the facing stones were painstakingly repositioned by hand to create a wider carriageway. RF603 began life as a country vehicle and lastly moved to Kingston for four months of service before withdrawal.

This June 1975 picture depicts RF351 in George Street at Richmond as it nears journey's end. Forty-five years later this view was virtually exactly the same, unspoilt by late twentieth-century architecture. Lilley & Skinner (footwear) was founded in 1835 and the company was absorbed by Stead & Simpson during the 1990s, which in turn passed to Shoe Zone in 2008. The building was home to Zara Home Furnishings by 2019 (ID).

CS Chiswick

RT1530 was new in August 1949 and was fitted with a Park Royal body. Its use as a PSV finished as early as 1969 when it was withdrawn from Poplar garage. It was subsequently used as a decimalisation trainer and a mechanical trainer before taking up residence at Chiswick Bus Works for use as a skid training bus. It is seen in use as such on the occasion of the works open day on 3 July 1983. It was bought by the London Bus Company of Northfleet in 2012 as a long-term restoration project.

CT Clapton

Having been in regular use at Catford garage, RT2406 was put into store at Clapton where it is seen on 29 May 1976, awaiting recertification. In July it returned to service at Romford where it remained until it was sold for scrap in March 1977.

FY Finchley

RT2143 saw quite a bit of service during the last years of RT operation. Prior to its stint at Harrow Weald (see page 14) it spent a few months at Finchley garage, where it helped out on the normally RM-operated route 26; it is seen in the garage on 17 July 1977. As previously mentioned, it later joined RT1530 at Chiswick as a skidpan bus.

Another capacity in which RTs were used in later years was as driver tuition vehicles. RT3028 last operated as a PSV vehicle from Battersea garage in 1970, following which it was transferred to Finchley for use as a training vehicle, a duty it performed on and off until 1979. It then passed into private ownership as a preserved vehicle and was photographed at Edgware garage on 21 February 1981 (ID).

H Hackney

RT2676 is seen in the company of RMLs Nos 2377/485 at Hackney garage on 17 July 1977. The Regent was new in August 1951 and was fitted with a Park Royal body. After moving between garages it was allocated to Sidcup in April 1963, where it stayed for the remainder of its working life. Withdrawn from PSV use in May 1977 it was acting as a staff bus when the above panorama was recorded.

HH Hemel Hempstead

RF115 was new to Grays garage in January 1952 and was one of 263 of the type that were initially assigned to Green Line duties. It is seen in Woodford Road close to Watford Junction station on 24 August 1974. Demoted to ordinary stage bus work it is working service 322 to Hemel Hempstead, which was its final home base. RF115 was withdrawn in February 1975 and sold to C. F. Booth at Rotherham for scrap.

HW High Wycombe

In the region of 870 RT Regents were newly assigned to the Country Division. Over the years buses were swapped between the Country and Central Divisions. RT3046 was first allocated to Reigate in February 1950. The remainder of its PSV career was spent at Leatherhead before it was moved to High Wycombe in November 1970 for driver training duties. It is seen in store at Stevenage on 25 February 1978.

HT Holloway

Holloway garage received half a dozen RTs in 1976/7 to help out on the normally RM/RML-operated routes of 14, 19 and 104. RT3911 was parked up in the garage yard on 17 July showing blinds for service 19. Having arrived the previous October, it was moved to Harrow Weald in November for use on the 140.

A significant number of RTs ended their days as driver training vehicles. RT2269 was allocated to Holloway garage for maintenance purposes and is seen some distance away in Potters Bar High Street on 19 February 1975. The car showroom had become a kitchen and bedroom shop by 2019 but the BP petrol station was still dispensing petrol.

T Leyton

Leyton garage received a small allocation of RTs in December 1976 to cover for the non-availability of RMs on the 230 route. RT531 is seen inside a packed garage on Sunday 30 January 1977. The 230 did not run on a Sunday so the full complement of six RTs was present at the time.

On a filthy day in March 1977, RT531 is seen making a U-turn in Seven Sisters Road for the return trip from Manor House station to Stratford. Behind the bus is St Olave's Church and the block of flats has since been refurbished and is now somewhat unrecognisable.

The 230 required five buses on Mon–Sat. RT Nos 2676 and 2554 are seen at the old Stratford bus station, under the multistorey car park, on 4 June 1977. This dingy edifice was demolished in the early 1990s and was replaced by a new bus station, which opened in November 1994. RMs returned to the route not long after this picture was taken.

L Loughton

At the start of 1976 Loughton garage was still providing RTs for routes 20^A, 167^A, 205^A (SuO) and 217^A. Following a reorganisation of bus services in the area on 10 April only the 20^A and 217^A remained. RT2844 is seen in Torrington Drive (off The Broadway) at Debden station on the last day of RT operation on the 20^A, on Friday 8 October 1976.

The 20^A was introduced on 19 May 1954 to serve the Debden estate. RTs took over from STDs some ten months later and remained the allotted vehicle type for the next twenty-one years. Ten buses were latterly required on a Saturday and RT3035 is seen outside Loughton garage on 29 June 1974. 'OPO' Fleetlines took over on 9 October 1976.

An allocation of Regents remained at Loughton until 19 August 1977 to provide buses for the 217[A]. RT1930, one of five buses allocated to the route on Mon–Fri, arrives at journey's end on 8 October 1976. The garage was closed in May 1986 and subsequently demolished. New houses now occupy the site.

A passenger on a 217[A] bus could enjoy a pleasant ride through Epping Forest, in the centre of which the bus would call in at the Wake Arms Inn (long-since demolished and replaced by a steakhouse). RT3951 makes a brief call at the Wake Arms on 29 January 1977 before continuing its journey through the forest to Enfield.

RT2268 was initially a country bus, but was first used on route 7 from Middle Row garage in July 1949. Two months later it was transferred to Northfleet. It was painted red in November 1965 and coincidently returned to Middle Row. Its stay at Loughton only lasted a few months as it was transferred to Catford within weeks of being photographed in Honey Lane at Waltham Abbey on 8 October 1976.

On 29 January 1977 RT2844 was photographed in Eleanor Cross Road (since pedestrianised) in the centre of Waltham Cross. The ultimate destination reads 'Loughton Garage via Golding's Hill'. The 217[A] was the last crew-operated route at Loughton garage and the route was completely withdrawn after 18 August 1977, with the only bus alternative between Waltham Abbey and the Wake Arms, immediately after that date, being the hourly Green Line service 703 until service 250 was introduced in March 1979.

Route 254 had an interesting history. It was first introduced on 18 January 1950 with pre-war AEC Regals (T class) that were based at the old Loughton garage. RFs were introduced to the route on 6 May 1953 and remained in charge until 10 April 1976 when AEC Swifts took over, only for the route to be withdrawn three years later. Seven buses were required on a Saturday when RF488 was captured outside the (new) garage on 29 June 1974.

Seen on 29 January 1977 at Loughton garage, withdrawn RT3295 is awaiting its fate. After twenty-six years of service for London Transport, the next journey for this particular Regent would be to the Yorkshire scrapyard of Wombwell Diesels. Since 1959 it had only ever worked from three garages – New Cross and Catford being the other two.

AD Palmers Green

Another Regent that had already run its last mile in service when photographed at Finchley garage on 17 July 1977 was RT4165. Officially shown as being in store at Palmers Green garage, it last saw service in 1975 at Norbiton garage where it was gainfully employed on the 65.

At the time this picture of RT3754 was taken inside Palmers Green garage, RTs had just finished on normal scheduled routes. However, this Regent is displaying evidence of having covered for an RM on the 298^A on or around 11 March 1978. RT3754 was put into store a few days later and had a short spell as a trainer before its inevitable demise.

In this view RT549 has just left Golders Green bus station and is seen in Finchley Road as it heads off for Chingford station. The 102 was a long-established route with which Palmers Green garage first became associated with in November 1947. By this date, 18 July 1977, the Mon–Fri allocation called for seventeen RTs while the route was operated by Routemasters on Sat/Sun and shared between Palmers Green and Muswell Hill garages.

RT219 waits to turn into Alexandra Park Road from Hatch Lane in the suburb of Muswell Hill in the second of a series of pictures taken on Monday 18 July 1977. Park Royal-bodied RT219 was one of the lowest numbered RTs still in service at the time and was in its thirtieth year of operation with London Transport. It was withdrawn the following February.

Above: RT2468 and RT2695 are seen laying over at the Chingford station terminus. Until January 1970 the 102 had been one of a number of routes that had terminated at the well-known Royal Forest Hotel at Chingford. The RTs finished on the 102 after 27 January 1978, but a number of the type remained at Palmers Green for a couple more months for the 261. In 2021 the 102 was plying its trade between Edmonton Green and Brent Cross while the petrol station in the background had by then changed into a car showroom. *Below*: RT2468 is seen in Hall Lane at Chingford Mount on its way to the station terminus. The Eastern Electricity Board offices had become the Wishing Well Pub & Eatery and an ornate clock had been placed above the centre window.

Above: RT3342 is seen coming off route on 18 July 1977 and turning off Green Lanes into Regents Avenue, which led to Palmers Green garage entrance. *Below*: RT3344 is seen at Muswell Hill Broadway on the same day. The splendid terrace of Edwardian buildings in the background was designed and constructed by James Edmondson (1857–1931) in the first decade of the twentieth century. This was also the local neighbourhood of Ray and Dave Davies, who were brought up in nearby Fortis Green and were founder members of the fashionable 1960s pop group the Kinks. The locality was immortalised in their album *The Village Green Preservation Society*. In the middle of the Broadway is a layover area for buses, while in the distance Our Lady of Muswell RC Church can be seen.

Service 34 ran for some distance across the north of the city from Barnet to Leytonstone and was shared between Palmers Green and Walthamstow garages. One of Palmers Green's input of seven buses on a Mon–Fri, RT1310, is seen in Leytonstone High Road, passing the Green Man PH (behind the photographer) on 18 July 1977.

The Leytonstone terminus of the 34 was alongside Harrow Green where RT2775 was photographed in the gloom on Friday 8 October 1976. In 2019 the building alongside was a Wesleyan Christian centre. RT2775 was bought for preservation in July 1977 and has been a regular attendee at events in recent years.

One of Palmers Green's stalwarts, RT3387 is seen outside Arnos Grove station on 8 October 1976. RT3387 spent over three years at the garage, first arriving in April 1974. It moved to Clapton garage as a trainer in September 1977 when the 34 was converted to 'OPO' with Daimler Fleetlines.

Following the conversion of the 102 to 'OPO' operation at the end of January 1978, the 261 still required seven RTs for the Mon–Fri schedule for a further five weeks. On 19 November 1977, RT637 was photographed alongside the Church of St John the Baptist in Barnet Wood Street. The 261 was first introduced in June 1961, running between New Barnet station and Arnos Grove station with just two Regents from Palmers Green.

The conductor of RT1310 is taking a quick cigarette break while chatting to the driver at the Chesterfield Road stand (junction of Bells Hill) in High Barnet on 8 October 1976. A lady can just be seen posting a letter and indeed Forbuoys newsagents has become Martin's convenience store, but still incorporating a post office, including the pillar box.

Still in Barnet and RT2695 is seen in Manor Road and is about to turn into Wood Street on a short working to New Barnet station, a journey of around fifteen minutes. Recorded on 19 November 1977, this Regent was sold for scrap the following month.

The first of four more pictures depicting RTs on the 261 on 19 November 1977 sees RT4281 on a garage journey (denoted as Palmers Green Cock) in Church Hill Road at East Barnet. The 'Cock' was a reference to the Cock Inn (Tavern) in Green Lanes, which was located opposite the garage and survived as a pub until 2010. Over forty years later this view was completely unchanged.

The 261 meandered its way north from Arnos Grove through the suburbs of Southgate, New Southgate, East Barnet and New Barnet to High Barnet, a journey of some thirty-five minutes or so. RT637 was heading for the northern terminus when photographed in Hampden Way, close to the junction of Mandeville Road.

Next to catch the photographer's eye was RT3410, which is seen in Hampden Way at Southgate, climbing away from Osidge Lane. The route went over to Routemaster operation from 4 March 1978, but these only lasted seven weeks as 'OPO' Fleetlines were introduced from 22 April. Complete withdrawal of the route was implemented on 26 September 1980 in conjunction with alterations to services 26 and 84.

Finally we see RT3342 in Waterfall Road at New Southgate with a journey bound for the garage (again denoted by Palmers Green Cock) beyond Arnos Grove station. It is passing the junction of Brookdale and the concrete bollard has either survived the test of time or been replaced, but it is still in the same position.

RT1312 was a spare bus for the 102 at the garage on 19 November 1977. This was the Regent's last operating base but it had certainly done the rounds during its twenty-eight year career with London Transport, having previously been allocated to no fewer than eleven other garages.

Although by the date of this picture, Sunday 27 March 1977, Palmers Green was still turning out RTs on three routes, there was no requirement for the type on the seventh day of the week. Consequently RT Nos 2488, 3344 and 3410, with a further six examples, are seen neatly parked among a number of Routemasters, the first of which is RM2123. The garage was still functioning in 2021 under the control of Arriva.

NS Romford

Buses terminating at Ilford would often display Ilford station, but the bus stands were located in the side streets on the north side of the railway. Route 139 was one of two routes that were still scheduled to be operated by Regents from Romford garage in 1976. RT686 is seen in Argyll Road at the Ilford terminus on 6 October.

For many years the 139 had run from Dagenham Dock to Gants Hill, but was extended to Ilford in June 1975. Its route from Ilford took it through Gants Hill, Chadwell Heath and Becontree Heath. RT2209 is seen in a rural setting in Billet Road at Chadwell Heath on 18 July 1977. It was delicensed later in the month and put into store at Potters Bar, but wasn't officially withdrawn until December 1978.

Seen at the same location and on the same day is RT2642. It has just turned into Rose Lane with The Harrow PH (still extant in 2019) on the right. This location presented a similar view more than forty years later with the presence of a mini-roundabout, in lieu of the central island, being the only change.

Although displaying Ilford Station, RT2209 is seen approaching the Dagenham Dock terminus in Chequers Lane on 6 October 1976. This was a somewhat desolate location, but at least the 139 had routes 145 and 148 to keep it company. Four decades later the building under construction had been demolished, while the lighting column had been replaced but without a street nameplate attached.

RT2295 is seen in Dagenham Heathway on 18 July 1977 crossing the junction of Reedle Road/ Parsloes Avenue. It is followed by one of Romford's Routemasters on either the 174 or the 175, both of which also terminated at Dagenham. The 139 was converted to 'OPO' with Daimler Fleetlines working from Romford garage just five days later, while RT2295 was moved to Loughton as a trainer before going for scrap in October.

The 175 regained an allocation of RTs on 4 September 1976, following a brief spell of operation by former BEA/BOAC Routemasters (RMAs). This resurgence lasted just six months when standard RMs took over. Despite the short period of operation RT2406 didn't escape the photographer's attention and was recorded at the Dagenham Ford Main Works terminus on 6 October 1976.

Route 250 was a long-established route from Hornchurch/Romford to Epping. It was worked by the TD class from 1948 until 1959 when RFs took over in July. Variously only requiring two to five buses, the RFs held sway until 24 April 1976 when Bristol LHs took over, only for the route to be withdrawn the following January. RF428 is seen turning from Victoria Road into South Street at Romford on 3 April 1976.

Central London

The initial Green Line Regal IV RFs, Nos 26-288, were placed into service on front line duties between October 1951 and July 1953. A further twenty-five RFs were converted for Green Line use in 1956. By the start of 1975 their ranks had been reduced to around 130 examples. RF179 was allocated to Reigate garage when photographed at Oxford Circus on 24 August 1974. The 711 ran from Reigate to High Wycombe calling at Banstead, Sutton, Mitcham, Tooting, Clapham, Oxford Circus and Uxbridge. This RF was deputising for a Leyland National LNC, the type having taken over in June 1973.

Other than the 109 and 155 services, which reached Victoria Embankment, the last truly central area route to be worked by RTs was the 176, which was fully converted to Routemaster operation on 21 March 1976. However, odd examples did continue to appear, as evidenced by RT422, which was turned out by Catford garage to work a duty on the 47. Normally employed on the 94, it is seen in Bishopsgate on 26 May 1978.

As mentioned above, the 109 just qualified as a central London route and continued to be worked by a mixture of RTs and RMs from Thornton Heath and Brixton garages respectively until 3 October 1976. RT2149 was recorded crossing a near deserted Westminster Bridge at precisely 1.30 p.m. on 14 August 1976, having just started out on its long journey south to Purley. When the route was first inaugurated in April 1951 the requirement was for a staggering eighty-eight buses on Mon–Fri from the same two garages.

In January 1977 there was a shortfall of serviceable Routemasters and RTs returned briefly to a handful of central London routes. The first of five views depicting RTs at work in Oxford Street on Monday 31 January sees RT4188 from Shepherd's Bush garage passing the House of Fraser while working on the 12 to Oxford Circus. At this time sixty-six RMs from four different garages were scheduled to work the 12 on Mon–Fri.

In this view Putney garage has turned out RT4631 to work a duty on route 30, which is working right through to Hackney Wick. This Regent's brief foray on frontline duty lasted four months, from November 1976 to March 1977, after which it was transferred to Palmers Green. Note how the sunlight has highlighted the misshapen lower-deck panels.

Meanwhile, on the same day Victoria garage had turned out a number of Regents to work their share of the 137 service (the route was shared with Norwood garage). RT4816 was captured outside Selfridges store on a part-route working to Sloane Square. It was one of five Regents drafted into Victoria as cover for Routemasters.

Another of Victoria's relief RTs was RT2602, which is seen nearing Marble Arch with a working to Clapham Common – still someway short of the ultimate destination of Crystal Palace. RT2602 had only arrived at Victoria earlier that month and continued in service until September when it was stood down for driver training duties. It did, however, see further service at Harrow Weald and Bromley the following year.

Finally, on 31 January 1977, RT3799 is seen heading for Archway station at Highgate. It is passing the junction of Hollies Street. The Dolcis footwear shop to the left of the bus was one of a number of stores owned by the long-established retailer. Founded in 1920 (but with roots back to 1863) the company went into administration in 2008. Ten years later the premises were occupied by River Island.

In 1977 there were just twenty N-prefixed night bus services, two of which were operated by Regents from Barking garage. The N98 ran from Victoria bus garage to Romford and RT595 is seen alongside the garage in Wilton Road in the early hours of the morning of 19 November 1977 with the 03.37 departure for Chadwell Heath.

AP Seven Kings

Seven Kings garage underwent an extensive rebuilding programme, which temporarily reduced the capacity of the building. On 29 June 1974, RT Nos 4433, 2565, 4135 and 2545 were to be found in the former coal yard alongside Goodmayes station, which was close to the garage. Three of the six routes then operated – the 86, 129, 139, 148, 150 and 193 – are displayed on the destination blinds.

While the 86 had lost its RTs in February 1976, the 129 was next to follow in October. RT4210 is seen on the York Road stand at Ilford on 6 October 1976 just three days before 'OPO' DMS Fleetlines took over. While this bus stand no longer exists, Barclays bank has since given way to the Punjab National Bank.

There was a separate stand round the corner in Argyll Road at Ilford to accommodate buses on service 139, which was only worked by Seven Kings on Saturdays. One of the five buses employed on the day, RT4624 was photographed on the Ilford station stand on 9 April 1977. The route was wholly worked from Romford garage with DMSs from July 1977.

Seven Kings shared operation of both the 139 and 148 with other garages. The Mon–Fri allocation on the 139 was provided by Romford as exemplified by RT2209, which has paused alongside Seven Kings' RT4433 at the remote Dagenham Dock terminus on 6 October 1976. Both of these routes lost their RTs on 23 July 1977.

RT4215 is pursued by an iconic Commer van along Cranbrook Road in Ilford on 9 April 1977 having just passed the junction of Coventry Road. The Commer van was introduced in 1960, with this particular example dating from 1971. Forty years later Rossi Bros was trading as the Titanic Café and Moss Bros (founded in 1851) – Suit You Sir – had become an internet and mobile phone shop.

On 18 July 1977, RT1762 was recorded in Parsloes Avenue in Dagenham, at the junction of Heathway. The two phone kiosks are of the K6 model, designed by Sir Giles Gilbert Scott and introduced in 1936, with the first of this series – the K2 – dating back to 1926. The more utilitarian KX series of kiosk, an example of which now stands at this location, was first introduced in 1982.

A number of bus routes had terminated at the Green Man Hostelry in Leytonstone for several decades; one such route was the 148 from Dagenham. RT4651 pulls on to the Green Man stand on 18 July 1977 already displaying the return destination. While the hostelry is still standing, renamed O'Neil's in 1995, the bus stand no longer exists.

Route 150 was first introduced in February 1947 running between Barkingside and Hainault. Its final incarnation while still worked by RTs was between Becontree Heath and Lambourne End (limited service) on Mon–Fri or Ilford and Chigwell Row on Sat/Sun. RT4126 waits to leave Becontree Heath bus station on 6 October 1976, bound for Chigwell Row. The Sat/Sun service had been converted to RM from 28 February 1976.

Apart from certain journeys that were extended to Lambourne End, the northern terminus of the 150 was adjacent to the Maypole PH at Chigwell Row. RT2430 (above) is about to depart the Orchard Way stand on 6 October 1976. While the actual stand was in Orchard Way, buses turned by using the pub's car park. RT2929 waits in Orchard Way while RT4625 makes the turning manoeuvre on 18 July 1977. The 150 was the last RT worked route at Seven Kings and was converted to 'OPO' with DMSs on 15 October 1977.

The weekday allocation on the 150 was for fifteen RTs from Seven Kings. RT2946 is seen in Green Lane at Goodmayes on 18 July 1977. Remarkably, the Silver Sea Chinese takeaway was still open for business in 2021, while René's hairdressing salon – and I shall say this only once – had become Express Cuts Unisex Salon.

Due to the confines of the garage building Seven Kings retained a 100 per cent allocation of Regents until 1976 when rebuilding works at the garage to accommodate larger vehicles was completed. RT4795 is plying its trade on the 193 in Goodmayes High Road in July 1976. Routemasters took over the service in March 1977 (ID).

RT4465 departs Seven Kings garage as RT4215 looks on in this July 1976 picture. The former was withdrawn later that month and was sold for scrap. The garage, located in Goodmayes High Road, was closed in September 1993 and the site is now home to a supermarket while a used car mart occupies the buildings across the road (ID).

S Shepherd's Bush

By 1976 Shepherd's Bush garage only retained a small allocation of RTs for its share of the 105, which was only required on Mon–Sat. RT4076 and RT953 are part of a trio seen on Sunday 23 April 1978, just one week before the route went over to RM operation. Fleetline DMS2274 is displaying a blind for the 220, the first DMS-operated service (ID).

The Shepherd's Bush stand for the 105 was outside the garage and RT2028 is seen on 9 October 1976 showing an ultimate destination of Havelock Estate, which was a bifurcation from the main route at Southall. Shepherd's Bush garage was opened in 1923; it was reconstructed in 1954 and was home to buses from the London United fleet in 2021.

HW Southall

On Mon–Sat the 105 was shared between Shepherd's Bush and Southall garages, with the latter providing two-thirds of the twenty-one bus allocation on Mon–Fri. RT1191 is waiting to depart Heathrow Airport bus station on 9 October 1976. This Regent was sold for scrap the following month.

In 1977 Southall garage (formerly Hanwell) was still providing RTs for three routes, the most significant of which was the 105, which ran between Shepherd's Bush and Heathrow Airport. Just nine years previously Southall had had a 100 per cent allocation of Regent IIIs. RT1777 is seen in King Street in Southall on 2 June 1977 heading for the airport followed by the ubiquitous Commer van. Rexone Chemists was still dispensing medicines in 2019 but under the name of Gill Pharmacy, which had also taken over the adjacent Tesco.

Another view at the airport, captured on 23 April 1978, sees RT2566 under the light and airy roof of the newly constructed bus station. Just a week later the RTs would be replaced by RMs and RT2566 would be moved to Bexleyheath for training duties.

Also seen on Sunday 23 April 1978 was work-stained RT4189, which is passing Shepherd's Bush Green as it nears the terminus in Wells Road (Shepherd's Bush garage). Only five RTs from Southall were scheduled for the 105 on a Sunday. As the 105 was the last of the Southall RT routes, RT4189 also went to Bexleyheath for use as a trainer.

The 120 was a more modest route, which ran from Greenford to Hounslow Heath via Southall and was scheduled for operation on a Saturday with seven RTs. Twenty-eight-year-old RT304 is seen in Barrack Road at Hounslow Heath alongside The Hussar PH on 9 October 1976. Two months later it was placed into store and sold for scrap in March 1977.

This southbound working from Greenford was only going as far as Norwood Green. It is 3 p.m. and RT590 glints in the low winter sunlight as it motors down Greenford Road, across the junction with The Broadway. The chemists in the background had turned into a centre for acupuncture and herbal therapy by 2019.

Generally, the northern terminus of the 120 was at Greenford station. Seen on 9 October 1976, RT1351 has then run out of service along Oldfield Lane North, crossed the Grand Union Canal and parked up in the yard of J. Lyons & Co., makers of Lyons Maid ice cream among other food products. The once extensive works was finally closed in 1998 and the area has gradually been redeveloped under the name of Greenford Quay.

The final view of a Regent on the 120 is of RT3865 in Greenford Road passing the junction of Costons Lane, again on 9 October 1976. The Sunday requirement was changed over to DMS Fleetlines on 1 October 1977, with full conversion to 'OPO' following on 28 January 1978. The shop Galleon Wine later became Solutions Ltd Windows & Glass.

The last of the trio of routes still operated by RTs from Southall in 1976 was the 274, which ran from Ealing Broadway station to Hayes station. While the driver sits in the cab, the conductor proudly poses for the photographer in front of their bus for the day – RT2196. Seen opposite Ealing Broadway station on 9 October 1976, this particular journey was only going as far as Yeading (White Hart).

Another short working on the 274 from Ealing sees RT1238 turning from Ruislip Road East into Greenford Road as it nears the Red Lion terminus on 4 December 1976. The 274 required seven buses on Mon–Sat, with no service provided on a Sunday. 'OPO' Fleetline DMSs were introduced on 1 October 1977.

Seen at the same location and on the same day but approaching from the west in The Broadway (Ruislip Road) is RT2566, which is doing the full length of the route. Regrettably, Arthur Edmond's Gentleman's Outfitters is no more and has been replaced by the Wishing Well eatery – ah well, I suppose food is more essential than clothes.

SE Stonebridge Park

On 27 May 1978, RF537 was found tucked away inside Stonebridge Park garage where it was undergoing recertification. Withdrawn from Kingston in June 1977, it was preserved by the London Transport Museum and now normally resides at the Acton premises.

These four Regents were parked in Kingston Coal Yard on 22 April 1978, but are included in this volume because two of them have northern connections. From the left, RT1608 (SE) and RT4714 (K) were both disposed of in June of that year, while RT563 (GM) and RT4286 (K) both survived as trainers until the following year.

V Turnham Green

RT273 assumed duties as a driver training vehicle at Hendon garage in October 1976. It moved to Turnham Green in April 1978. On 25 August it was recorded quite close to home when it was photographed in Chiswick High Road. The green is on the right at the junction of Town Hall Avenue.

UX Uxbridge

By 1976 there were no RTs allocated to Uxbridge, but the garage was still responsible for turning out RFs on the 223 and 224/224[B]. On Saturday 9 October 1976, RF384 is seen at the Heathrow Airport end of the 223. The vehicle requirement was for eight RFs on Mon–Fri, seven on Saturdays and five 'OPO' Fleetlines on a Sunday. LCBS Leyland National SNC188 is waiting behind on the 724 to Staines while an RT on the 105 can also be seen.

At the other end of the route RF513 was photographed on the Bakers Road stand in Uxbridge on 4 December 1976. As part of a large redevelopment scheme in this part of Uxbridge during the 1980s a Travelodge Hotel was built directly behind the bus. The 223 was converted to Fleetline operation on all days of the week just eight days later.

Seen on the same day at Uxbridge station is RF519 on the 224. Running between Uxbridge and Laleham, five RFs were scheduled on Mon–Sat, with no service provided on a Sunday. The route was converted to operation with AEC Swifts at the same time as the RFs were ousted from the 223. Both RF519 and RF513 briefly lived to fight another day, the former at Kingston and the latter at Hounslow. Alas, Leathercraft no longer exists, but No.4 Windsor Street does and is now occupied by a hairdressing salon, a watch repairers and an employment agency. The bus station has also been altered out of all recognition.

GM Victoria

RTs were widely used as driver tuition vehicles throughout the 1970s. This particular example, RT2673, was allocated to Victoria Gillingham Street when photographed in The Pavement at Clapham Common on 21 July 1978. While the Cut Above has changed to the Counter Culture Eatery, the street nameplate remains attached to the wall.

WW Walthamstow

Walthamstow garage contributed eleven buses to the running of the 34 on Mon–Fri. RT206, a 1947 example that had been new with a Park Royal roofbox body, was captured at the western end of the route in Barnet High Street (A1000) on 8 October 1976. The terminus was, and still is, near to the junction of Fitzjohn Avenue. Largely unchanged, the route was worked from Palmers Green garage by Arriva in 2021.

On its journey from Leytonstone RT4558 would pass through Leyton, Walthamstow, Edmonton, Arnos Gove and Totteridge & Whetstone. The Regent was recorded in Totteridge High Road on Sunday 17 July 1977. The Sunday allocation was for just three RTs from Walthamstow assisted by two RMs from Palmers Green.

RT206 is seen again in the garage yard at Walthamstow on 17 July 1977. Walthamstow was originally a tram depot, which was opened in June 1905. It was then converted for use by trolleybuses in 1936. These in turn were superseded by Routemasters in 1960/1. The garage's only scheduled involvement with RTs was for route 34, which lasted from January 1964 (route gained from Leyton) until September 1977 (converted to 'OPO'). The garage was a victim of privatisation in 1994 and has since been replaced by new housing.

WN Wood Green

A number of RT training vehicles were allocated to Wood Green garage for maintenance purposes. RT2150 is seen with one of Enfield's allocation of Routemasters, RM403, at the northern outpost on 25 November 1978. RT2150's stint as a trainer was short-lived as the Regent was withdrawn two months later and sold for scrap.

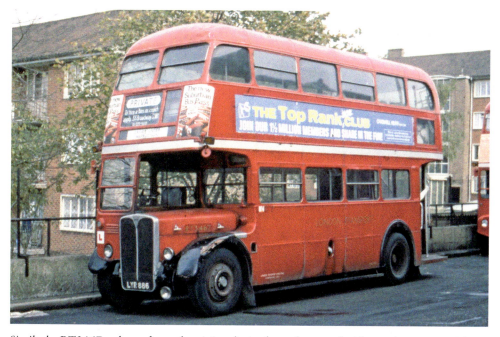

Similarly, RT3467 only performed training duties for a short spell. After seeing use as a PSV at Harrow Weald, Catford and Barking garages throughout 1978 it was moved to Wood Green in October for use as a driver training vehicle. It also went for scrap with RT2150. It is seen at Muswell Hill garage on 4 November 1978.

RT3828 had a long career as a trainer. Records show that it did very little proper bus work after December 1966. In and out of storage, it was used as a decimalisation currency trainer in 1970. Various stints as a driver trainer then followed before its final move to Wood Green in July 1976. It is seen at Muswell Hill garage on 4 June 1977.

BK Barking

At the start of 1976 Barking garage had the second highest number (Seven Kings just topped it) of RT buses north of the Thames. At the time these were employed on routes 62, 87 and 148. RT3894 is seen at the remote Dagenham Kent Avenue (Ford Main Works) terminus with Fleetline DMS689 (on the 145) for company on 6 October 1976.

Route 148 ran from Leytonstone Green Man to Dagenham Ford Main Works or Dagenham Dock. The route had a shared allocation with Barking garage providing six RTs on Mon–Fri and three on Sundays. Seven Kings had a daily contribution including the full complement on a Saturday. Two views taken on 18 July 1977 depict RT1983 (above) in Green Lane at Goodmayes and RT678 (below) in Bennetts Castle Lane at Becontree. All the individual shop premises seen in the upper view had been amalgamated by 2019 to form the Eden Pharmacy. Five days after these views were recorded the 148 was converted to 'OPO' using Fleetline DMSs with operation of the route entirely undertaken by Barking. The route was withdrawn after 19 March 1993.

The 87 ran in two overlapping sections, with all duties covering the section of route between Becontree Heath and Barking. RT4021 is passing Becontree Heath bus station on 6 October 1976 having commenced its journey at Harold Hill. The B178 referred to on the road direction sign is now the A1112 and the Dartford crossing is via the M25 bridge.

This trio of Regents was captured at the Blakes Corner terminus of route 87. Seen in Linton Road at Barking on 2 September 1978 are RT Nos 4069, 939 and 4515, all of which have their blinds set to return to Harold Hill Dagnam Park Drive. Twenty-eight buses were employed on this route from Barking garage on Mon–Fri, while the Sunday allocation called for six RTs from Barking and four RMs from Romford.

Nearing journey's end on 9 April 1977 is RT4180. Heading for Blakes Corner it is seen in Longbridge Road, approaching Barking station. The Halifax, seen immediately left of the bus, had become a Cash Converters by 2019 (still looking after your money, of sorts). RT4180, which was originally a green country bus, lasted in service at Barking almost until the end of RT operation on the 87.

At the other end of the route, in Abbey Wood Lane at Rainham, RT Nos 4255 and 4320 catch a few rays of sunshine as they wait under a threatening sky for their return departure times to Becontree Heath. In 2021 this was the terminus of routes 165 and 287.

Seen on 2 September 1978, RT1654 has just dropped off a passenger in Dagnam Park Drive at Harold Hill; it will then turn right into Leamington Road and left into Petersfield Avenue before turning back into Dagnam Park Drive where the layover point was opposite the square. RT1654 didn't quite last until the end and was withdrawn in March 1979 (ID).

Level crossings in London were somewhat rare and even more so one carrying four tracks. RT4515 is seen crossing the Barking to Tilbury via Rainham railway in Ripple Lane on 29 January 1977. The crossing was later replaced by an overbridge, although the block of terraced houses/shops was untouched by the bridge works. Devon Road, opposite the white car, is now accessed from a lower level road below a concrete retaining wall.

Two pictures of RTs at the Harold Hill terminus but seen at different locations. Prior to December 1966 the 87 had run to Brentwood but was then diverted to serve Harold Hill, with the terminus in Hilldene Avenue, close to the junction of Gooshays Drive. From August 1969 the Sunday service was extended to Dagnam Park Drive and then from July 1977 it was altered to terminate opposite Dagnam Park Square, on all days of the week. RT678 and RT4021 (above) are seen in Hilldene Avenue on 6 October 1976 while RT4627 and RT3951 (below) are reposing in Dagnam Park Drive on 2 September 1978. A bus lay-by has since been constructed at the latter location, which in 2021 was the terminus of route 174, with the 87 having been cut back to Romford in March 1993.

The 87 effectively had four termini. The buses that commenced their journey at Becontree Heath ran beyond Barking through Rippleside and Dagenham to Rainham. The Abbey Wood Lane terminus was somewhat out of the way and ideal for the crews to take their extended break. RT Nos 939, 4320 and 4255 were doing just that on 6 October 1976. Nothing had really changed in 2021 other than the concrete road had been given a tarmac overlay and a lay-by had been provided for services 165 and 287.

The crew of RT1522 take a breather at Becontree Heath bus station on 6 October 1976 before heading back to Rainham. At the time the bus station also played host to central area routes 23 and 25 and more local routes 150 and 173. A new development known as Trinity Place was under construction on this site in 2019.

Inside Barking garage on 2 September 1978. *Above*: RT3467 is on the left, RT3254 is alongside the fuel pumps, RT3408 is to the far right, and the back end of RT2293 second from the right. The back of Fleetline DMS693 is also visible, along with RM2135, which at this time would probably have been present for type familiarisation (with the type making a return after an eight-year absence) (ID). *Below*: The garage was also a changeover point for crews on routes 62 and 87 and RT Nos 2773, 2293 and 2816 are all on layover between duties. In the days of the RTs and RMs the drivers had to possess an element of athleticism to be able to climb into the cabs of these buses. The sliding cab door was also essential for close parking of the vehicles.

RT1562 is seen in Upminster Road South in the centre of Rainham on 9 April 1977. According to the clock tower the picture was captured at precisely 2.50 p.m. Rainham Clock Tower was unveiled on 7 November 1920, with the complete edifice having been constructed as a memorial to those who lost their lives in the First World War.

It is Saturday 3 April 1976 and RT701 is leading RF461 along Romford South Street. The Regent was withdrawn from Barking in January 1977, while the Regal moved from Romford to Hounslow later that month following the conversion of the 250 to Bristol LH operation on 24 April.

Barking garage was the crew changeover point for buses going in each direction. These two Regents are heading for the extremities of the route, with RT1798 going to Rainham and RT4515 making its way to Harold Hill. From the following day, 28 October 1978, this routine was undertaken using Routemasters.

Also seen on the same day making a crew change outside the garage is RT3467. The pronounced camber of the road resulted in the buses leaning at an acute angle. The following day RT3467 moved to Wood Green (see page 67) for a short spell of driver training duties.

Bridge Road in the centre of Rainham on 9 April 1977 and RT3407 is ready to return to Barking garage while RT2461 is running through to the terminus in Abbey Wood Lane. The road layout has changed somewhat at this location and the pavement has been widened to cover the area of the bus stand. The funeral directors is now dead and buried and the shop is today a hair and beauty salon called Guys and Dolls.

Another last day scene and RT2773 is seen in Romford South Street waiting for the lights to change at the junction of Eastern Road as it heads home to Barking. Looking somewhat battered on the lower panel this would be the Regent's last day in PSV use as a short spell as a driver tuition vehicle followed before a final trip to the yard of Wombwell Diesels the following June.

A busy scene in Romford South Street on the last day of RTs on the 87 sees Leyland National LS120 passing RT1989. Route 248 worked out to the eastern extremity of Upminster. The clock records that the picture was taken at 4 p.m. The building housing Collyers Furnishers has since been replaced by an incongruous brick structure and the ABC cinema has also been lost in the mists of time.

RT1989 again, later that evening, and all is not well as a garage fitter sits in the cab with the bonnet up. Anxious-looking passengers wait for the prognosis: will the bus have to be taken out of service or not? Unfortunately, yes, and it was replaced by RM319.

Two pictures taken at the Abbey Wood Lane terminus on the last day of Regent operation. RT2150 (above) reposes on the stand in the morning while RT2750 (below) occupies the same spot after nightfall. Both buses were withdrawn on the day. While RT2750 was another that met its end in Yorkshire, RT2150 escaped the cutter's torch, literally, as it was bought for further use while at Wombwell and is now preserved.

Barking garage, in Longbridge Road, was opened in 1924 to cater for the expansion of bus services in the area; it was extended in 1931. There is an expansive open yard on the east side. In 1978, Barking still had a sizable allocation of Regents to cover its combined Saturday requirement of thirty-six buses (one additional vehicle on each route on Mon–Fri) for routes 62 and 87. *Above*: RT595 with Bow garage's trainer RT2972 on 2 September. *Below*: RT3407 heads a neat line of fourteen Regents parked up on 22 April (ID). The garage was still going strong in 2021 under Stagecoach ownership.

Seen at Barking garage on 27 October 1978, RT2816 has just run its last mile in passenger service and the blinds have been removed. Next up for this Regent was a period of storage at Loughton before its inevitable demise in Yorkshire.

RT3408 had the honour of working the very last RT duty on the 87. It is seen in the early hours of Saturday 28 October 1978, suitably decorated and about to depart Becontree Heath for the short trip back to Barking garage.

RT851, minus its bonnet number, is seen over one of the inspection pits inside Barking garage on 2 September 1978. It is possibly receiving a check on the oil and coolant levels. Note the wordage 'COACHMAKERS', painted on the blue door.

RT4181 was caught on camera in Longbridge Road, at the junction of Ventnor Gardens, on 2 September 1978. Route 62 went down in history as the last route to be worked by RTs. The Saturday allocation was for nine buses. In the early 1970s the route was almost a complete circle running from Ilford to Barking via Hainult and Chadwell Heath (ID).

Another view taken on 2 September 1978 sees RT379 9, previously allocated to Bromley, about to turn from Ripple Road into East Street, in the centre of Barking. This manoeuvre is no longer possible as East Street has since been pedestrianised. While the buildings to the left and behind the bus are still extant, all those to the right have gone to make way for the Vicarage Field shopping centre.

RT1301 has paused to pick up passengers at the Lindisfarne Road bus stop in Valence Avenue at Becontree on 27 October 1978. RT1301 made it to the end and was used on the last day of RT operation before being exported to the United States.

Sometimes the photographer has to brave the elements to get that all important picture. RT4555 was recorded at the Gascoigne estate terminus on 6 October 1976. The 62 (to Marks Gate) still serves this stop, while there is now a modern industrial estate where the concrete panel fence stands on the left.

RT624 on the penultimate day of RT operation, 6 April 1979, at the Chigwell Row terminus of route 150. It has never been explained why this journey worked to Chigwell Row – perhaps it was to commemorate the route from its 1940s/1950s days (ID).

The penultimate day of RT operation, Friday 6 April 1979, was a somewhat dull but mainly dry day, but the photographer was not deterred as evidenced by the following pictures. RT624 and RM370 (on the 86) were caught laying over in Wangey Road at Chadwell Heath. RT2541 is just visible in the distance.

RT624 is seen again, having just dropped off some passengers at the stop outside No. 8 Upney Lane in Barking. More than likely the travellers would be unaware that a significant chapter in the history of London's buses was about to come to an end.

RT1790 has stopped outside Chadwell Heath station and only has a short distance to go before it turns round for the trip back to Barking. This scene is virtually unchanged except the small building behind the bus now has an upper floor level. The station was opened in January 1864 by the Eastern Counties Railway.

Also only going as far as Chadwell Heath is RT2541, which has paused to pick up passengers outside Barking station. Ten buses were allocated to the route on Mon–Fri. This is another scene that has changed very little over the intervening forty years.

From March 1977 the normal Mon–Sat route of the 62 was from Barkingside via Hainult, Marks Gate, Chadwell Heath and Becontree to Barking Gascoigne estate. The route was extended to Creekmouth on Sundays. RT2240 is first seen descending Station Road at Chadwell Heath (above) and then turning from Gale Street into Woodward Road at Becontree (below) on its return journey. In the upper view the road has since been reconstructed and a footway provided on the left-hand side. This Regent was one of the six turned out by Barking garage the following day for the grand finale. Following its moment of glory, it went on to greater and higher things (literally) as it was rebuilt as a triple-decker to represent the purple bus that appeared in the Harry Potter series of films.

Two views taken in New North Road at Hainult depict buses travelling in opposite directions. RT1798 (above) has not far to go before it reaches Barkingside. Forty years on Hainult Drapery had become a dry-cleaner, while Hamilton's Bakery, on the corner of Lancelot Road, had turned into a mini supermarket. On the opposite side of the road RT1790 (below) is just setting off from the stop at the junction of Kirby Close; Hainult London Underground station, which is situated on the Central Line loop, is adjacent to the overbridge in the distance. Both of these Regents entered service in the summer of 1950 and both have survived into preservation.

RT1798 (above) was later photographed while making another trip to Barkingside. One passenger has alighted as another two have boarded the Regent at the Canonsleigh Road bus stop in Woodward Road at Becontree. Travelling in the opposite direction is RT2671 (below). A prospective traveller in 2021 would still be able to catch a 62 bus at this location, but would only be able to travel as far as Marks Gate, and on a Stagecoach Enviro 400 type bus at that. This was to be RT2671's last day in service as it was not part of the last day activities. It was exported to the United States that July and the author has not been able to find any subsequent record of its fate.

So the last day dawned, Saturday 7 April 1979, with a hint of sunshine. The driver and conductor of RT2541 are seen in conversation at the Barking Gascoigne estate bus stand. The Regent never made it to Chadwell Heath and was replaced by a Routemaster at the garage. There is now a modern-day industrial estate on the land beyond the concrete fence.

As forty years of RT operation is only hours from coming to an end, RT2240 was captured turning from Ripple Road into East Street, in Barking town centre. This section of East Street is now known as Station Parade. In the distance a Routemaster can be seen in London Road working a journey on route 23 to Becontree Heath (ID).

Above ans left: Running in normal service, RT624 initially did a short trip to Chadwell Heath Valance Avenue (above) where, following a brief stop, it turned back for Barking. Its last trip in public service took it through to Barkingside (left ID), from where RM208 duplicated the duty for its return trip to the garage. The driver of the RM and a youngish-looking inspector are deep in conversation, but I guess it will never be known what was being discussed.

RT624 is viewed from a different angle in Barkingside High Street. RM208 has now pulled in front of the Regent and an inspector is guarding the platform. Meanwhile a large gallery of photographers eagerly capture the moment for posterity.

RT624 is now making its final trip back to Barking garage. It is seen turning from Billet Road into Rose Lane at Marks Gate; the Harrow PH is on the right. Following close behind is an unofficial entourage of cars and privately owned buses – mainly RTs.

Suitably decked out, RT624 passes along Upney Lane on the last leg of its final journey. A handful of onlookers stand on the pavement to witness the occasion while three over-enthusiastic passengers must have had a rush of blood to their heads.

RT3251 was not used in service on the last day but did take part in the final cavalcade. Suitably fitted with a special blind, it waits inside the garage for its cue to line up outside. Fortunately, this Regent, which was a country Green Line bus until 1972, also survived and is now preserved and in 2020 was part of the Ensignbus Hire Fleet.

All revved up and ready to go. RT Nos 4633, 2671 and 1798 are preparing to leave the garage for the grand cavalcade. The garage foreman is making a final check on the leading vehicle (ID).

RT Nos 2541, 4633, 2671, 1798 and 3251 have lined up alongside the garage in South Park Drive while a constant procession of what would now be deemed as vintage cars drive past the waiting buses in single file. Two Bobbies (no high-visibility clothing) oversee proceedings.

Preserved 1939 AEC Regent RT1 leads the procession from South Park Drive into Longbridge Road. Enthusiasts and ordinary bystanders watch on in admiration as the buses make their final appearance for London Transport.

RT624 has now joined the rear of the cavalcade directly from the garage, and the final picture sees the procession retreating along Longbridge Road, bringing to a close forty years of operation of the type. A small number of Regents continued to be used as driver training vehicles for a couple more years.